French Kisses Last Forever

Poems

by Liza B

REGENT PRESS
Berkeley, CA

Copyright © 2013 Liza B.

ISBN 13: 978-1-58790-258-1
ISBN 10: 1-58790-258-3

Special Author's Edition

This is #_____ of 25 copies

Printed in commemoration of
REMEMBRANCE OF THINGS PROUST
presented by Radio Proust
Saint John's Presbyterian Church
Berkeley, California
November 14, 2013

REGENT PRESS
Berkeley, California
www.regentpress.net
regentpress@mindspring.com

May each page of this
art poetry book
draw the reader
into its universe —
each poem extremely different
but connecting to what
is most profound
in all of us
LOVE

Liza B.

Profound Quietude

In an Arabized decor
Close to a fragrant patio
Lascivious, she abandons herself
Her body drifts
An erased sun
Brushes her
A cadenced breeze
Whispers
Soft crumple
Her senses are becoming distant
But she does not sleep
Her eyes become sugary
Her hair archipelago
Marries the lace
She has for sheet the sky
And a sacred alcove
Her breath diaphanous veil
Rhythms the slow dilemma
Thus her life wilts
But death is unscathed

For You

My frivolous hair
Brown blond halo
My sweet mutineers eyes
Painted with mascara
My greedy mouth
With offering lips
My slender neck
With subtle senses
My velvet fingers
And my love palms
My pink breasts
With erected points
My marked waist
And my arched back
My very soft belly
With the taboo door
My cello hips
And the silk of my skin
My infinite legs
Topped with lace mesh

Windows

With its large wound of infinitude
Persists this remaining feeling
Immortal challenge of incompleteness
Twisted by the absence of a lover

You are here without being here
And me I want to be reborn
I have in me this antiquated hope
To live in other latitudes
To escape forever the habit
And to hinder all weariness
You are here without being here
Maybe a sentinel
Of my future well being.
I want a life with an apricot taste
Of the unpredictable
I want a caramelized life
Fruited, leafed, winged, azure, rasberrized
Nothing denatured
A life of patios and fountains
Of lattices and trains
A life earth and sun
Innocence and awareness
The hammock
And the surf
The quietude
And the plenitude

Drunk of Nature
To live with absoluteness
To relive exquisitely
Undulate and meander
And the discretion of the wind
Full of lace
You are far without being far
You are here without being here

Failure and Aromatic

Taste of insomnia on your shoulder
Pepper and coriander
Cinnamon breasts, flexible willow back
Meandering of mingled legs

Hoot of emotion
Flower of chilli

Grain of curry craziness
Strand of insolence on your paprika lips
Soft clove, cumin and turmeric
Furry ginger love

Cascading music and Gothic sky
Languishing heart of starred anise
Saffron navel chalice
And anarchic vanilla mouth

Offense caress
Delicacy

Don't forget love burns
Love bites
Love dies
A sprig of thyme extinguishes

Appoggiatura

And why not
The shadow of your guitar
On my black stockings
Like a sun that stings
And tattoos my skin
Everything remains enigmatical
And distorts the tempo
But why not
The shadow of your guitar
On my black stockings
This spurred thought
Bridles my violin
And one thousand times furrowed
My vinyl frets
Insolent picador
With a tenor's look
You pierce my body
Your glittering spurs
Shooting the lace mesh
Skim the nylons
And screech on the veil
Of my black stockings
In the shadow of your guitar

Fierce Night

In the pond fringed with mottled sassafras
cast a tender and surreptitious dream
soft volute
shaggy haired idea
the dressed eye polished up his kris
and the pale moon tarnished the iris

Sacrificial sleepiness
Artificial indolence
I live in my night
The skiff of my thoughts glide
On the pond fringed with mottled sassafras
Where my dream rushed by
Near me suffers a snuffer
The lightning sighs sulfur

Enemy night
Insomnia night
The low tide of my reveries renounces anchoring
My drifted body begs to sink
Frantic calligrapher, my heart quests the inkwell

My page is laughing a fief
The biting of my words dodges kieff*
The dagger of my eye gleams more and more
In the pit of my soul cries a gazelle
Trying immensely to temper the gall
The evanescent dawn had a taste of sky
Three hours of night
Three days of rain
Three months of emotions
Offer me an armful of jasmine, lilacs, syringa
At the border of pond fringed with mottled sassafras
Where an gazelle fell asleep

* Turkish word indicating a state of absolute restfulness

Capri

Island in the Bay of Naples

In the favor of harmony
Easily gets erased
The decorum
Alcove with a taste of Italy
Curtains-birds, blown heat
Provide some intimacy hours

Sugary looks
Honey lips
Slightly acid skins
Kisses of sky

Algorithm of words-thought
Of body to heart
Of revealed life
Of heart to body
Of chills and sweats
Of desires and again

Black laces to please
Precarious high heels

Mutineers and cunning cuddles
"Galvanized" "Hackneyed" intertwined
To utter the sacred phrase
Grip on destiny?

The words gradually work their way
To hang at the wet lips of kisses
The air freezes; cloud-emotion
The mad humor of love imposed itself
What's the matter the words existed

"See you soon" galvanized
"See you soon" hackneyed

Night in His House

In the background a saffron robe sky languishes
Dissolutes with a tender purple of uncertain contours
Without the proud and haughty knight noticing
Flat brilliance of vigor with soft reflection of bronze

I unhook my knight
Hungry for dreams

In the white frame an unusual obelisk stands
Pleasant symbol of ugly and immodest reality
Unique too grey tower erected
towards the horizon
Which is taunting me and spying on me
with its painted eye

I conjugate my anxieties
In the present and the past

In the foreground the books with offering pages shake and shout
to me
the antiquatedness of love,
of humor and of the desperate prayer
While the vegetal hair at length
Unravels revealing reluctantly its leaves
in between the lace of the macramé

I tame the nausea
I underline the disgust

My eyelid infinitely heavy stamps
the pictorial details stolen by night
To train a thought that scatters
And my disheveled soul beset by sad torments

The knight finally saw me
Then I close my eyes.

Exorcism

The dune buried the mysteries
And after having shaken itself my charred soul
Perceiving the purple destiny of filigree
Came aground on a trivial beach

Pinned to my memory remains a scent
But where still bloom the fragrant phloxes?
Then the memory of an oriental madder silk fades
Poisonous flower unfaithful as soon as the equinox

Pinned to my memory arpeggios resound
Of a burning passion with a crimson belly
Defoliating all the emotions of the anthology
And all the characters which the man incarnated

Pinned to my memory rises the narcissus
Mirror without silvering revealing a ghazal
In the heart the bitter taste of licorice
On the skin the rough sensation of sisal

At the delta of my mind the meanders hoarse
While my entire body awakens rebelling
Unfastening the pins, stabbing the knots
Vomiting the absurdity: life is a circular scheme

The dune buried the mysteries
And after having shaken itself my charred soul
Perceiving the purple destiny of filigree
Came aground on a trivial beach

Exorcisme

La dune a enseveli les arcanes
Et après s'être échouée mon âme arcane
Apercevant le destin pourpre de filigranes
Est venue s'échouer sur une plage anodine

Fibule à sa mémoire demeure une fragrance
Mais où donc embaument encore les phlox ?
Puis s'estompe le souvenir oriental d'une soie garance
Fleur vénéneuse infidèle aussitôt l'équinoxe

Fibules à sa mémoire résonnent les arpèges
D'une passion brûlante au ventre incarnat
Effeuillant toutes les émotions du florilège
Et les maints personnages que l'homme incarna

Fibule à sa mémoire s'érige le narcisse
Miroir sans tain dévoilant un ghazal
Dans le cœur le goût âcre de la réglisse
Sur la peau la sensation rugueur du sisal

Au delta de ma pensée s'éparpillent les méandres
Tandis que mon être entier s'éveille rebelle
Dépatant les fibules, poignardant les malandres
Vomissant l'absurde : la vie est un diallèle

La dune a enseveli les arcanes
Et après s'être échouée mon âme arcane
Apercevant le destin pourpre de filigranes
Est venue s'échouer sur une plage anodine

Illusions of Arabesques Foams of Thoughts

My Oval Heart

Blow a hollow sun on your kneeling soul

set with infertile dust and raw-boned, Unhook
the boat of your purple gloved night and
swallow the beauty of the infinite journey. Shout

an outraged silence shrouded in cheerful Praise and
dream a disappointed and exhausted spray of Light.
Perfume the iris or the helianthemum and caress the
yataghan that threatens the hypogeum and also flatters the nightjar.
Offer armfuls of clouds bicolor Zephyrs Hallowed with musk that
surprises the abstract, Awaken

Your dawn surreptitiously and slowly
Decimate your sublimations plotted of subterfuges and Ocher
derisions.
Be grandiloquent Stamp and burn This winter heart
that pulverizes in the Distance period

Sustine and Abstine

The salty water of my eyes refrains from divulging
The river of my blood is listening to the wounds that are turning blue
Under the fingernails of my reason splints groan
The summer of my wounded heart whispers a fruitless orchard

All the sounds of my life muffled
I nailed the clouds

A flask exhales softly an evening rose garden
The amber window of my roof inhales the south west wind
On a vanilla pod exhales a wintery dawn
Meanwhile withers away an effluvium of disarray

All the perfumes of my essence evaporated
I tied up the wind

In the hollow of the tawny iris hidden gold lived
Watering down all the outlines of the tattooed look
In my eye is printed the wounded shadow of a sycamore
Meanwhile on my walls tarnishes rip a mirror

All the images of my dreams are effaced
I stare at the sun

The expression of my cheek caresses the hard brilliance of a sapphire
My aching limbs seek to embrace a baobab tree
And my lips fringed with purple brush the elixir
My frozen fingers pinch emphatically an ultimate nabob

All the prints of my ring fingers are wiped off
I threw vitriol in the sea

The chlorine of the passions left a taste of flat notes
And on the fire of desire a samovar hisses and suffuses
Distilling slowly the aroma of an exorable randomness
On the wrinkled table cloth the savoriness of a frivolous supper twinkles

My taste buds forget the flavor
I bit the light

How important my five senses
How important my five stanzas
As without love I barely exist

九月十九日

我想去看你。我想我们的想相同。我笔你有空见。明天见。你有两下子。省省吧！不工作狂。善有善报。我可以给你打电话吗？你是我的爱人，一起电来电。你很可爱。你的眼睛很美。我为你疯狂。陪我好吗？我要你。亲我睁开眼睛。我想做爱。你喜欢我的乳房摸我。怕什么？你做得很好。

Liza B.

TAMBOURINE

Again and again
This wave of nausea
The tam-tam of my heart
Gently mats
And the futile trace
Of my recent lover
Is drawing indelibly
In the wrinkle of the time.

When the moons of the soul
Get full of water
Where is my hero?

Intoxicance

To wait for sunrise . . .
While the greedy time
swallows greedily the instant
and mistreats the body

While around shimmer
temptations
Promise of going astray

While it only remains a link
abstract thoughts
subtle messages
wild memories

While an ocean of storms
Affronted and rocked
stride over our destinies

To wait for sunrise . . .
Apnea break
Before returning to the breath
Carrier of life

Before our bodies
Will be again united
and unique
Before our senses
Regain their sense
Make quiet love and its impatience
In order it swells with impertinence
and pertinencies

Reassure my love and be there
I'm so afraid of time
And I want to die with elegance
Without any regrets and deprivations
Thanks to you only

Eucharist

Everything was only symbiosis,
symphony or syntax
and also
heavy breasts full of meaning
breasts for the senses
Wet with cologne
and aesthetic kisses

Intimate diving
Eyes and caresses
To the ultimate center
Delicacy.
Mouth of supreme water
Lips applied
Pleasure distilled
along the erected desire
Extreme voluptuousness

Chalice-delight
Union-communion
Tuned bodies
Accomplice thoughts.

Everything was only scarlet
A mutual fugue that suddenly bursts
beyond us, birth in the other.
Almost to faint or to die.
Life transferred.
The feminine in him feeling the masculine in her.

Completeness Infinitude Fullness

The rarity of the moment gives birth a feeling
of breathlessness and of words born free
of the united unison of sensual harmony
He was her She was him, religiously united
in an epitome of the Eucharist.

"We can go no further."
Were his words of the moment.
With a sixth sense she knew forever
That this sentence had two meanings.

Vanitas Vanitatum

Bruised sun, pale moon, withered tree
Extreme poem
Orange flowered, supreme bird, nestled heart
Cream song
Strange paradise, beautiful angel, wrinkled bed
Blued mirage

Where is living the equinox?
Where is born the paradox?
Where blushes the phlox?

When is the dawn concealed?
When does the again ripen?
Vanitas Vanitatum
Et omnia vanitas

www.ingramcontent.com/pod-product-compliance
Lightning Source LLC
Chambersburg PA
CBHW041220070526
44584CB00001B/29